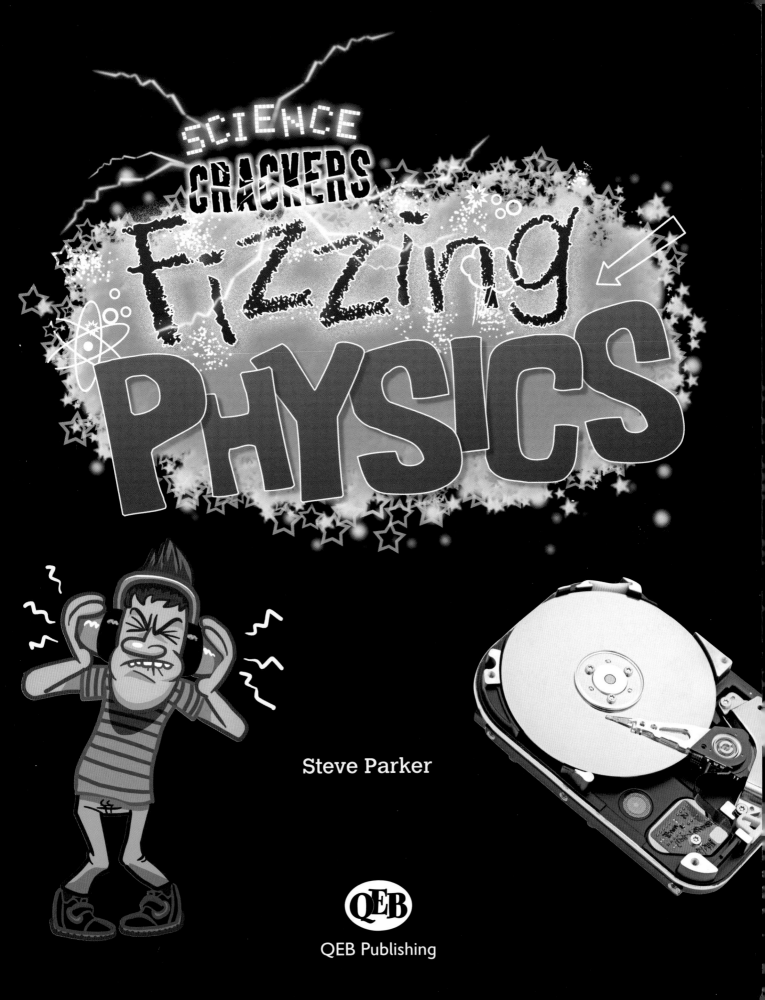

SCIENCE CRACKERS

Fizzing PHYSICS

Steve Parker

QEB

QEB Publishing

Created for QEB Publishing by Tall Tree Ltd
www.talltreebooks.co.uk
Editors: Rob Colson and Jennifer Sanderson
Designers: Jonathan Vipond and Malcolm Parchment
Illustrations, activities: Lauren Taylor
Illustrations, cartoons: Bill Greenhead

First published in the United States in 2011 by
QEB Publishing, Inc.
3 Wrigley, Suite A
Irvine, CA 92618

www.qed-publishing.co.uk

A CIP record for this book is available from the Library of Congress.

ISBN 978 1 60992 037 1

Printed in China

Picture credits
(t=top, b=bottom, l=left, r=right, c=centre, fc=front cover)
Alamy: 17c Myrleen Pearson; **Corbis** 12b New Sport, 26br Gavin Hellier/Robert Harding
World Images; **Creative Commons** 17t and 31 Brian Gratwicke, 18tr Rob Shenk;
Dreamstime 18bl Elena Elisseeva, 19cl Kiselev Adriy Valerevich,; **istockphoto** 23br
Embosser; **Shutterstock** 1 and 27t Ragnarock, 2 and 6t Regien Paassen, 4bc Gluestock,
4bl Elisanth, 4tr Sergey Lavrenter, 5t Andrew Horwitz, 5c Rena Schild, 4br Rynio Productions,
6b Brett Mulcany, 7b Gilmanshin, 7 Greg Epperson, 9c Robert Spriggs, 9b Chen Wei Seng,
10b Matt Jones, 10–11 Sergey Utkin, 11tr Yuriy Zhuravov, 11b and 23 tr Daniel Gale, 12t
Scott O Smith, 13l Eric J Enger, 13tr Sascha Gebhardt, 14l Antony McAulay, 14r daphne,
15t vlue, 15bl hj schneider, 16b Ferenc Szelepcsenyi, 16t Adisa, 19cr Olaf Speier, 19b Sergei
Butorin, 22 Kevan O'Meara, 23bl Olga Besnard, 23 bl Vitezslav Halamka, 23cr Gordana,
23br Tatiana Popova, 23 cr ps-42, 25bl valzan, 25bc loriklaszio, 25 br gresei, 26t Awe
Inspiring Images, 27b Vibrant Image Studio, 27b dubassy, 28c 13848535, 28r Yuri Arcurs,
28b Filatov Alexey, **SPL** 17r Andrew Lambert Photography, 19tr Joe McDonald/Visuals
Unlimited, 28 Alex Bartel

Note
Website information is correct at time of going to press. However, the publishers
cannot accept liability for any information or links found on third-party websites.

In preparation of this book, all due care has been exercised with regard to the activities
and advice depicted. The publishers regret that
they can accept no liability for any loss
or injury sustained.

The practical activities in this book have been
checked for health and safety by CLEAPPS, an
organization that provides practical support
and advice on health and safety in science
and technology.

Words in **bold** are explained
in the Glossary on page 31.

CONTENTS

MACHINES EVERYWHERE 4

GO AND STOP 6

ON THE SLIDE 8

LIGHT AND DARK 10

SEE THE LIGHT 12

COLORS GALORE 14

STOP THAT NOISE! 16

FAST, HIGH, AND LOUD 18

BOTTLE PANPIPES 20

BUCKET DRUM 21

THAT'S ELECTRIC! 22

POTATO POWER 24

MYSTERY MAGNETS 26

USING MAGNETS 28

MAGNETIC FISHING 30

GLOSSARY 31

INDEX AND FURTHER INFORMATION 32

MACHINES EVERYWHERE

It is a hot day and you need an ice-cold drink. You have a bottle of soda, but its metal top is fixed on very hard. Using a bottle opener, you lever it off.

A bottle opener is a type of machine, called a lever. It lets you move something using a big **force**, but only a small way. Another simple machine is the wheel. You can roll a heavy load on it without too much effort. Ramps or steps are also simple machines. They let you move something upward in small, easy stages.

PLAY MACHINES

A playground has machines, not for work, but for fun. A seesaw is a lever and a merry-go-round is a type of wheel. There may be a pulley on a rope, too.

Simple Machines

The main simple machines are ramps, wedges (such as an ax blade), wheels and axles, screws (right), pulleys, gears, and levers. A ring-pull tab on a drinks can (left) is a lever. You can combine these simple machines to make more complicated ones. For example, a wheelbarrow (above) has levers for handles as well as a wheel.

REPAIRING MACHINES

When your bicycle breaks, you might use a simple machine to repair it. To tighten a nut, you need a wrench. This is a type of lever. It moves a nut a small distance, but with a great deal of force.

IMAGINE THIS...

Machines make jobs easier! Imagine what your life would be like if you did not have machines to help you.

WHEELS

The wheel is the ideal machine for rolling things along. You do not have to lift anything, you just push or pull. You can also use wheels on bicycles to zoom along quickly and easily.

GO AND STOP

IMAGINE THIS...
If something moves fast then suddenly stops, it can be damaged or harmed. This is why people wear seat belts in cars.

Many machines, from cars to jumbo jets, give you the force to keep moving. Their force comes from engines, but there are also natural forces that can move us, such as **gravity**.

Some forces, such as friction, or rubbing, make us slow down and stop. You can feel friction when you rub your finger against a rough surface—your finger will not slide easily over the rough surface. Friction can make things difficult to move. But it can be very helpful at keeping us in one place and in slowing us down.

FORCE OF GRAVITY
One force that works everywhere on the Earth is gravity. It pulls things downward. On a downward slope, such as a roller coaster track, gravity makes the roller coaster speed up.

SHOWING MOVEMENT

At an air display, the smoke trails from planes show how they move. They climb, turn, and go up and over and down in a circle, a move called looping the loop.

LIFE-SAVING FRICTION

Without friction, climbers would fall off steep rocks. Climbers test each hand grip or foothold to make sure there is enough friction so that they can cling on.

USEFUL FRICTION

Most of a motorcycle's working parts are smooth, hard, and well-oiled. But not the brakes! They press on the wheel brake disk to cause friction and make the motorcycle slow down.

ON THE SLIDE

Friction is the force that stops your plate sliding off your meal tray. Try this to see for yourself how friction works.

YOU WILL NEED:

- large plastic meal tray
- protractor
- small book
- old cell phone
- bar of soap
- pen
- piece of paper
- cooking oil
- roll of paper towels
- few dozen small marbles

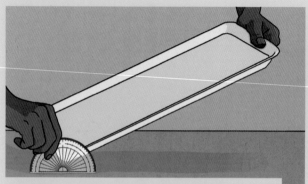

1 With the tray on a flat table, lift one end slightly. Practice measuring its angle with the protractor. A friend can help by looking at the angle from the front.

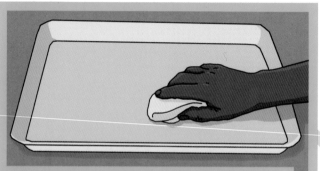

3 Put some cooking oil on some paper towel and smear the tray with the oil. Repeat step 2. The objects that stay on the tray at the highest angle have the most friction.

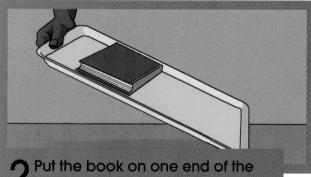

2 Put the book on one end of the tray. Slowly lift this end of the tray until the book just starts to slide. Write down the angle of the tray. Do this for the cell phone and soap.

4 Clean the tray. Put the marbles on it. Balance the book on the marbles. How does this change the angle at which the book starts to slide? Are the marbles more effective than the oil at reducing friction?

Uneven surfaces

Layer of oil

Layer of oil reduces friction between the two rough surfaces

Every surface, even the smoothest, has tiny bumps and pits. The bigger these are, the more they rub and scrape past each other, and the greater the friction. Adding oil reduces the amount these bumps and pits rub together, and this lessens the friction.

SMOOTH RIDE

Objects roll more easily than they slide. Placing small balls between surfaces reduces friction because the balls roll rather than slide. Inside many machines, such as the wheels of a race car, metal balls, called bearings, are used to reduce friction and keep the machines working efficiently.

MUBADALA ABU DHABI

Santander

ETIHAD

Santand

LIGHT AND DARK

Darkness can be scary, especially if you do not know what is around you. Light is much better. Your eyes can see the shades, colors, and patterns that surround you.

Things that give out light are called light sources. For us on the Earth, the brightest light source is the Sun. Substances that let light rays go through them, such as glass, are called **transparent**. Substances that stop light passing through, such as wood, are called **opaque**. Light rays travel in straight lines and cannot curve around objects, so on the far side of an opaque object is a dark area known as shadow.

DAY AND NIGHT
Sunlight travels through space before it reaches us. As the Earth spins, the part of its surface facing the Sun has day, while the part facing away has night.

NEED FOR LIGHT
Many animals need bright light to see their surroundings. Tropical fish come from warm places where the Sun is usually bright and strong. They need a powerful light in their tank so that they feel at home.

SPOOKY SHADOWS

The dark shape behind an opaque object is called its shadow, or umbra. The shadow is the same shape as the object that is blocking the light. This can be a lot of fun when putting on a shadow puppet show!

MAKING LIGHT

When the Sun sets and it gets dark, we can make our own light by flicking on a light switch. Electricity flows through a light bulb, causing it to glow and give out light, turning darkness into light.

SEE THE LIGHT

You see light sources, such as an electric bulb, because they give out their own rays of light. These travel through the air and into our eyes. However, chairs, trees, people, and books do not give out their own light. So how do people see them?

Objects that are not light sources bounce back, or reflect, light that hits them. This is how you see them—by the light they reflect. If there is no light source, these objects would have no light to reflect, so we would not be able to see them.

MIRROR IMAGE

When you look in a mirror, you are seeing a reflection, which is a flipped image of yourself. If you raise your right arm, it looks like your image is raising its left arm.

REAR VIEW

Mirrors help you to see behind you. Race-car drivers wear helmets and are strapped in, so they cannot look over their shoulders. They have to use their rearview and side mirrors.

MOONSHINE

The Moon does not make its own light. You can see it because it reflects sunlight. As it goes around the Earth, the Moon appears to change shape as the amount of its sunlit part that we see on Earth changes.

IMAGINE THIS...

A flat, shiny surface produces a reflection. Curved or bent surfaces reflect the light rays in a different way, so the image is an odd shape—which can be funny.

STILL WATER

The surface of still water is like a smooth mirror that reflects light from the scene into our eyes.

13

COLORS GALORE

Most people like rainbows, but where do they come from? Ordinary white light from the Sun, a lamp, or a flashlight is made of a mixture of all the colors of the rainbow. These are called the spectrum. Follow these steps to see them.

As white light travels from one substance to another, such as from the air into a glass prism or a raindrop, it bends, or refracts. Each color refracts by a slightly different amount, so the colors separate to form a spectrum.

1 Next time it is both sunny and raining, look for a rainbow. Rainbows are formed by raindrops scattering rays of light.

2 Look at a DVD's blank side near a bright lamp. Twist and turn the DVD until you see a spectrum. You can probably angle it to see more than one spectrum!

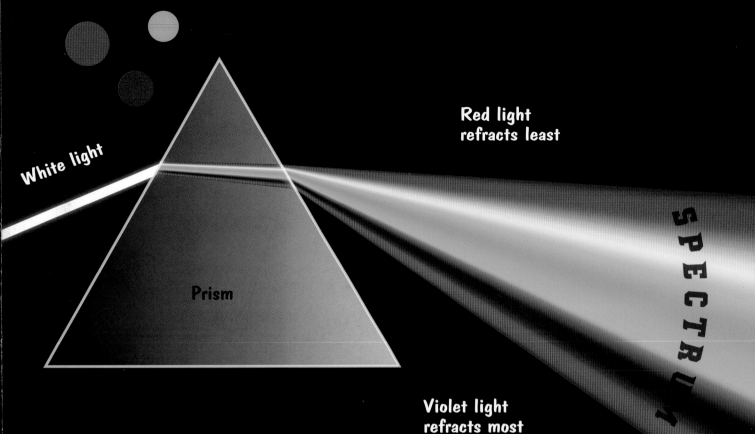

White light

Prism

Red light
refracts least

Violet light
refracts most

SPECTRUM

3 Next time you walk past a puddle, check it out for rainbow colors. They are usually caused by a thin layer of oil floating on the surface.

4 In a dark room, shine a flashlight through a clear glass of water onto some black cardstock. Angle the beam of light to produce rainbow colors on the cardstock.

STOP THAT NOISE!

People sometimes say: "It is so noisy, I can hardly hear myself think!" Loud noises can confuse people, while other sounds can be pleasant and relaxing.

Sounds travel through the air as sound waves. A sound comes from a source such as headphones, a television, an engine, and your own voice. A sound source must shake back and forth quickly, known as **vibrating**, to make its waves.

Sounds that we like and enjoy can be made by musical instruments or birds or people singing. Noisy sounds, such as traffic or jet planes roaring past, dogs barking, vacuum cleaners, and fire or burglar alarms are unpleasant. We usually want them to stop.

ANNOYING SOUNDS

Some sounds can be unpleasant. Loud, harsh sounds, such as noisy traffic, make us screw up our faces and put our hands over our ears to keep them out. After a while, they put us in a bad mood.

MAKING MUSIC

Some sounds, such as those from the instruments in an orchestra, go well together. All kinds of objects can be used to make musical sounds, from hoses to trash cans!

ANIMAL SOUNDS

Animals use sounds to send messages. Dog barks can mean "Beware!" A bird's song can be used to show off its lovely voice. Frog croaks and grasshopper chirps can often say "Let's play!"

Frogs croak to attract mates

HUMAN SOUNDS

Everyone can be a sound source in a number of ways. You talk, shout, and sing using the voice box in your neck. You can use other body parts to make sounds. You can clap your hands and stamp your feet, and even whistle.

VIBRATE

Something must vibrate to produce a sound. This can be the vocal cords inside your voice box or a string on a guitar. As it vibrates, it squeezes and stretches the air next to it, starting sound waves that move out.

IMAGINE THIS...

Male humpback whales sing long and beautiful songs to attract female humpbacks. Their songs can be heard by other whales hundreds of miles away.

FAST, HIGH, AND LOUD

SOUNDS FAST!

Sound waves move through the air at about 1,115 feet (340 meters) per second. When jet fighters roar through the air faster than the speed of sound, they are called supersonic.

Sound waves travel through the air like waves traveling through a slinky (below), squashing and then stretching the air in succession.

The loudness of a sound is called its **volume**. If the radio is too quiet, you turn it up using the volume control. Whether a sound is high or low is called its **pitch**. This can range from the high cheep of a bird to the deep boom of thunder.

Wavelength

Whisper 20dB

HIGH AND LOW

The pitch of a sound depends on the **wavelength**—this is the distance between each sound wave. The shorter the wavelength, the higher the sound.

TOO HIGH FOR US

Noises that are too high-pitched for us to hear are called **ultrasound**. Bats find their way by making ultrasonic squeaks and listening to the echoes that bounce off objects.

Loud shout 80–90 dB

Chainsaw 100–110 dB

Bomb exploding 200 dB

QUIET AND LOUD

The loudness or volume of a sound is measured in decibels (dB).

19

BOTTLE PANPIPES

You can make your own musical instruments from throw-away or recycled items around the house. Make your own panpipes and blow your audience away with a good tune.

2 Put some water in one bottle and see how it changes the sound, making it higher in pitch. You may have to change how hard you blow.

1 Put the bottles in a row next to each other on a table. Blow across the top of one of them to make a hooting sound.

3 Put increasing amounts of water in the bottles along the row. In each bottle, there is less air to shake, or vibrate, so the note is higher.

4 If you have a guitar or piano, adjust the water to "tune" the bottles. Now you are ready to play!

BUCKET DRUM

Once you've made the bottle panpipes, you can build a drum kit and form your very own junkyard band.

YOU WILL NEED:

- empty food and drink cans of different sizes
- two large spoons
- old bucket (metal is best)
- tape

1 Tap each can with a spoon to hear the pitch of the sound it makes. Put them in order from lowest to highest pitch.

3 Using your spoons as drumsticks, beat out the main rhythm on the bucket and add in faster taps on the cans.

2 Turn the bucket upside-down. Tape the cans in order around the bottom of the bucket, level with the bottom of the bucket.

You could make a "guitar" with a shoebox and rubber bands. You could also tap a row of glass jars or bottles with different amounts of water in them to make a xylophone.

THAT'S ELECTRIC!

Electricity powers our modern world. It can be sent long distances along wires and it can be used in many ways, from lights to motors, radiators, and sound equipment.

Only some substances carry electricity. They are known as electrical **conductors**. Most of these are metals. Copper and silver are especially good conductors. Water is also a good conductor. Substances that do not carry electricity are called electrical **insulators**. They include wood, plastic, cardboard, fabrics, and pottery or ceramics.

IMAGINE THIS...
Batteries might be handy and portable, but make sure that you use the right batteries for each appliance.

POWER PLANTS
Electricity is made in power plants. Some power plants burn fuel such as coal, oil, or gas. This turns water into steam, which spins turbines to generate the electricity. Wind farms (above) use wind to spin turbines.

DANGER!

Wires, cables or power lines on big towers and pylons, and machinery such as transformers, all carry very strong electricity. You should never mess around with these, or with the plug sockets in your home.

HIGH

Grid
400,000 volts

HOW MUCH?

The strength of electricity is measured in volts (v). Voltages range from very low-powered batteries to very high levels in overhead power cables.

Household power
220-240 volts

PORTABLE POWER

Batteries make electricity from chemicals. They power small moveable gadgets, such as toys, cell phones, music players, and flashlights. They can also be used to power large devices, including cars, such as this Tesla Roadster. Instead of using gasoline, you plug a battery-powered car in to recharge before zooming off again.

Batteries
1.5-12 volts

LOW

Tesla Roadster

POTATO POWER

Batteries make electricity from the combination of chemicals inside them. You can do the same using a potato!

YOU WILL NEED:

- two big fresh potatoes
- two short pieces of thick copper wire
- two **galvanized** nails
- two crocodile clips
- insulated wire
- light-emitting diode (LED)

1 Number the potatoes 1 and 2. Push a nail into each potato, most of the way down. Insert a piece of copper wire into each potato, as far away from the nail as possible.

2 Using the clips and insulated wire, connect the nail in potato 1 to the copper wire in potato 2.

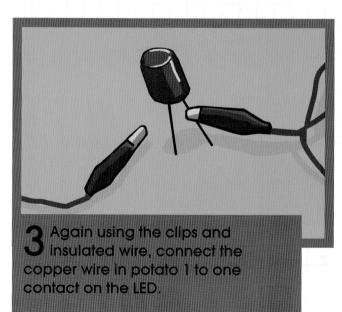

3 Again using the clips and insulated wire, connect the copper wire in potato 1 to one contact on the LED.

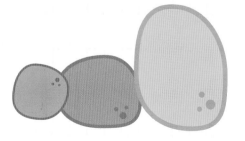

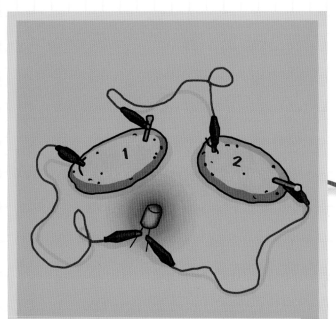

Potatoes contain chemical energy. In the potato battery, the zinc on the galvanized nail, the chemicals in the potato, and the copper in the thick wire, all react together to make an electric current.

4 Finally, connect the nail in potato 2 to the other contact on the LED. When you do this, you make a complete circuit, and electricity starts to flow. The electricity will make the LED glow.

Add more potatoes with their nails and copper wires to the circuit. Make sure you connect the nail of one to the copper wire of the next. Does the bulb glow brighter? Try fruits such as cucumbers, tomatoes, apples, and bananas. Which one works best?

This device can measure the electric current of different objects— including fruit!

MYSTERY MAGNETS

One of the strangest forces cannot be seen, but can push or pull with huge power. This mysterious force is magnetism, and it is used in hundreds of machines.

Magnetism particularly affects iron objects. Steel is mostly iron, and is used to make many items, from silverware to refrigerators. Magnets stick to these objects. A magnet has two poles where its force is strongest: one pole is North (N) and the other is South (S). When two magnets come close together, if their poles are "like" or the same, they push apart, or repel. Two different or "unlike" poles pull together, or attract.

FLOATING MAGNETS

Some trains use magnets to zoom along. A magnet underneath the train pushes against a magnet on the tracks with so much magnetic force that the train actually floats! This type of train is called a maglev train, which is short for "magnetic levitation" (lifting).

MAGNETIC FIELD

The force of a magnet acts in an area called the magnetic field. The field curves around between the poles of the magnet. You can see this by scattering iron filings around a magnet. The iron filings will line up in the pattern of the magnetic field.

MAGNETS AND INFORMATION

Information is stored on computer hard disks as patterns of tiny magnetic spots. A hard disk is usually a stack of metal circles, each with a very thin magnetic coating.

IMAGINE THIS...

The main law of magnetism is like poles repel and unlike poles attract. So...

N + N = REPEL
S + S = REPEL
N + S = ATTRACT

COOL MAGNETS

Small, button-shaped magnets with plastic covers can hold notes to a steel refrigerator casing. The magnetism passes through thin paper, but is much weaker with thicker paper or card.

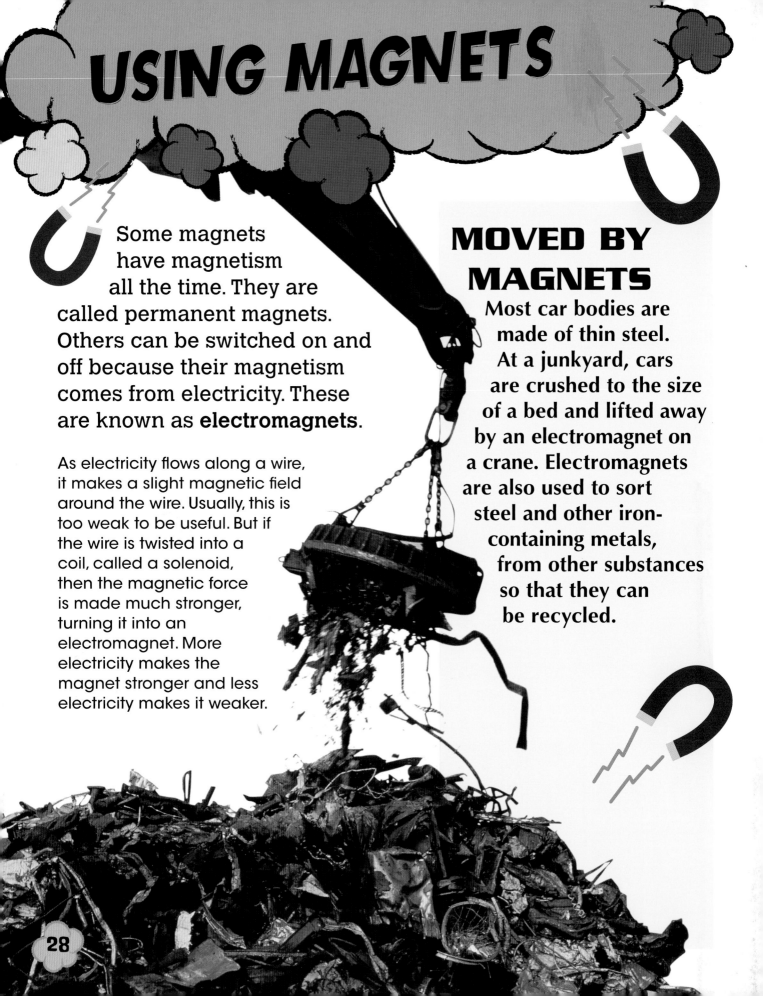

USING MAGNETS

Some magnets have magnetism all the time. They are called permanent magnets. Others can be switched on and off because their magnetism comes from electricity. These are known as **electromagnets**.

As electricity flows along a wire, it makes a slight magnetic field around the wire. Usually, this is too weak to be useful. But if the wire is twisted into a coil, called a solenoid, then the magnetic force is made much stronger, turning it into an electromagnet. More electricity makes the magnet stronger and less electricity makes it weaker.

MOVED BY MAGNETS

Most car bodies are made of thin steel. At a junkyard, cars are crushed to the size of a bed and lifted away by an electromagnet on a crane. Electromagnets are also used to sort steel and other iron-containing metals, from other substances so that they can be recycled.

MAGNETS IN MOTORS

Electric motors contain wire coils that spin around inside permanent magnets. The coils use electromagnetism to pull and push against the permanent magnets. This produces a turning force, which makes the motor spin.

Wire coil spins when electricity passes through it

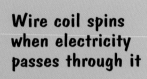

MAGNETIC SOUNDS

Headphones make sounds when magnetism vibrates a tiny sheet inside them called the diaphragm. Louder sounds are produced when the magnetism is stronger and vibrates the diaphragm more.

IMAGINE THIS...
People rely on dozens of electric motors, from electric toothbrushes to washing machines, dryers, vacuum cleaners, and food blenders.

NAVIGATION

A compass is a magnetic needle that spins around to line up with the Earth's natural magnetic field, and points North and South.

MAGNETIC FISHING

You can discover which substances are magnetic and try your hand at fishing at the same time!

YOU WILL NEED:

- string
- wooden spoon
- strong magnet
- pencil
- cardstock
- scissors
- tape
- variety of small objects

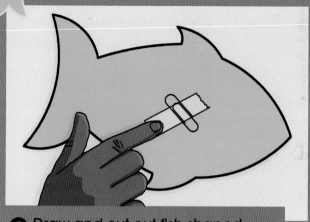

2 Draw and cut out fish-shaped cardstock. Tape a small object to each fish.

3 Go fishing! Try to pick up each fish one by one with the magnet. Which objects stick to it best?

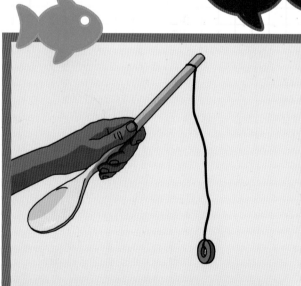

1 Tie string to the end of the spoon and around the magnet to make a "fishing rod."

Substances that contain iron, such as steel, are attracted to magnets. Paper clips, nails, and bolts should work well. Thumb tacks and metal fasteners may work—but they could be made of other metals.

GLOSSARY

CONDUCTOR
A substance that carries electricity. Copper is a good electrical conductor.

ELECTROMAGNET
A device with an iron core surrounded by a coil of wire. When electricity passes through the coil, the core is magnetized.

FORCE
Action on an object that causes its motion to change speed or direction. Gravity and friction are types of force.

GALVANIZED
Coated with zinc.

GRAVITY
A force that attracts objects to each other.

GRID
A system for distributing electric power throughout a region.

INSULATOR
A substance that does not carry electricity.

OPAQUE
Describes a substance that does not let light pass through it. Wood is opaque.

PITCH
How high or low a sound is.

PRISM
A transparent object that breaks up light into the different colors of the rainbow.

TRANSPARENT
Describes a substance that does let light pass through it. Glass is transparent.

ULTRASOUND
Sounds with such a high frequency that humans cannot hear them.

VIBRATING
Moving back and forth or up and down very quickly and repeatedly.

VOLUME
How loud or quiet a sound is.

WAVELENGTH
The distance between one peak or trough of a sound or light wave to the next peak or trough.

INDEX

air 12, 14, 16, 17, 18, 20
animal sounds 17

ball bearings 9
batteries 23, 24–25

chemicals 23, 24, 25
compasses 29
conductors 22
current 25

day and night 10
decibels 19

Earth 6, 10, 12, 29
echoes 19
electricity 22–23
   grid 23
   household power 23
   light 11, 12
   motors 29
electromagnets 28
engines 6
eyes 12
forces 4, 5, 6–7, 23, 26, 29
friction 6, 7, 8–9
fuel 22

gears 4
gravity 6

insulators 22

levers 4, 5
light 10–11, 12–13, 14
   rays 10, 12, 13
   sources 10, 12
light bulbs 11, 12

magnetic field 26, 28, 29
magnets and magnetism
   26–27, 28–29, 30
   poles 26
metals 4, 9, 22, 25, 26, 27,
   28, 30
musical instruments 16,
   20–21

opaque 10, 11

pitch 18, 19
prisms 14
pulleys 4

rainbows 14
ramps 4
reflection 12, 13
refraction 14

screws 4
seeing light 12–13
shadows 10, 11
simple machines 4–5
solenoids 28
sound 16–17, 18–19
   speed 18
sound sources 17
sound waves 16, 17, 18
spectrum 14–15
Sun 10, 11, 14
sunlight 12

transparent 10
turbines 22

ultrasound 17

vibration 16, 17
vocal cords 17
voice 16, 17
voice box 17
volts 23
volume 18, 19

wavelength 18
wedges 4
wheels 4, 5, 9
wind farms 22

FURTHER INFORMATION

http://spaceplace.nasa.gov/en/
kids/projects.shtml
fun and amazing projects on physics.

www.sciencekids.co.nz/physics.html
Information, projects and games on
things to do with physics.